Clutch

Clutch

Zora Howard

Penmanship Books
Brooklyn, New York

Penmanship Books

Published by Penmanship Publishing Group
593 Vanderbilt Avenue, #265
Brooklyn, NY 11238

Copyright © 2010 Zora Howard

Cover Design by Rico Frederick

All rights reserved. This book may not be reproduced in whole or in part (except in the case of reviews) without written permission from author.

"The Comparitive Clause" first appeared in City Limits Magazine.
"Dear Son" first appeared in The Spoken Word Revolution Redux (edited by Mark Eleveld).
"Biracial Hair" first appeared in Connect.Politic.Ditto. (Urban Word NYC anthology) and was featured in a short film by Lisa Russell and Governess Films that won a NY Emmy Award.

First Penmanship trade edition: November 2010

To contact
Zora Howard please visit www.penmanshipbooks.com.

ISBN# 978991095
Printed in The United States of America
10 9 8 7 6 5 4 3 2 1

For You and

You and

You,

hiding,

yeah, You too.

Contents

Laughter in my Hood, Enmanuel Candelario   9

Revolutionary

January 22nd, 2009   13

Our Insurance

Block Party   19

Biracial Hair   20

The Border   23

Something   26

The Anatomy of a Fatback   28

Black Music   30

Dear Son   32

1953 Cadillac Coupe DeVille   35

Children   38

Stage   40

Beginning   45

Shooting. Stars.

Mating Call   49

The Comparative Clause   51

Hard Core; Track 16   53

A-Train Sisterhood	56
Daydream	59
Favor	61
Walking	63
Chichos	67
In Love	68
Joy	70
M-18	72

Clutch

Letter	75
Vaseline Colored	77
Firstly	79
Play	81
Hush	83
Who Dat Dey Ring Dem Bells For	86
They've Cut Down All the Trees on Convent	88
Another Poem About	92

Laughter in My Hood

I love the sounds of Sundays in my hood.

An open pump,

Children laughing—

    Uncontrollable,

        Contagious,

           Sin berbuensa laughter.

Like life can't get any better laughter.

From the bottom of ya belly.

This laugh is only heard in my hood.

Ok, maybe your hood too.

Laughing

Rainy sunny,

Noses runny,

With no money,

Like the hood does

When shit ain't funny.

    —Enmanuel Candelario

Revolutionary

Little girl spirit
is sometimes big and small and
sometimes not at all.

January 22nd, 2009

Let me be the little girl
> again.

With feet all too big for her sandals. Size 9.
Age 9.
> again.

Flesh like a boomerang.
Scabbed knees.
Purple shins.
I-don't-need-the-helmet skin.
> again.

Plant me, lily, and I will break through your wood.
I will shame your rose. Past your rows.
Thirteen.
Front teeth piano keys. Cheeks.
Cheeks.
Budding, weak,
but budding nonetheless.
"Do you have another size, my body don't fit."
When it don't fit.
> again.

That stage was bigger than my world.
Little girl,
lot of people.
People,
make me disciple.
> again.

Learn me how to teach
humbly
or teach me how to learn
lovely.
A place created for
bowlegged beauties.
Exclusive:
For the oil sheened only,
exceptions made for the butterfly

with the one afro-puff
smack
dab
in the middle of
her head,
I would like to be a part
       again.
A pen with a fluffy feather
at the end.
That wrote in a sugar gel
with glitter.
There,
we did not yet know how to lie to ourselves.
There,
everything other than the truth
sounded funny.
What I put on paper
was necessary.
      I want to write in gel pen.
        again.
Pink and purple journal,
sparkles,
if you do not mind,
I'd like to reintroduce myself.
I am,
possibly,
not quite the same as you remember me.
This place
may be too sacred
for the scribbled circles my poetry
has become.
But,
here's a go:

Dear Me,
I still think you are very pretty
and smart.
I do not want you to change a thing

about your face.
It is very important to have a big heart.
Other things don't matter as much,
says God.
I love you very much and mommy and daddy and Alex and God.
Sincerely,
Me.

P.S. Happy 16th Birthday.
P.P.S. Your hair looked really cute today.
P.P.P.S. I love you. I wanted to tell you.
        Again.

Our Insurance

Mama always says
that all she gotta do is
stay black and then die.

Block Party

Auntie has pressed her four stomachs through the child bars and is calling for you to *bring your black ass inside and finish sweeping this floor* before it gets dark.

All the other sistergirlfriends are skipping in the yellow paint construction squares marking the block like they are something of a children's game and less than the blueprints for a city that won't belong to us.

The Blueprint is playing out of Apt. 4B's kitchen and Rayshawn, Raydon, Rajon, and RaeRae stand in a clump on the corner, undulating to a Bobby Blue Bland sample.

There is a court made of chalk and trashcans that is more a promenade of Accolades, Chukkas, Spizikes, and Huaraches than a presentation of Alley Oops, Cross Overs, Spin Moves and Hook Shots.

Above, a fire escape collective of smoke rattles the building as it breathes. All the uncles settle their backsides in lawn chairs low to the ground and hover over a used-to-be-crate-of-wine-coolers spread with jacks.

The little ones dance in a rainbow of government owned water with only their diapers. Men in blue come to fasten the hydrant one last time, until finally they give up.

Mr. Ron, or as he prefers to be called, DJ Big Brother Rock, will play *Sweet Thing* tonight, will play *Through the Fire* tonight, will play *If I Were Your Woman* tonight, will play *Got to Give It Up* tonight, will play *Purple Rain* tonight, will play *Como La Flor* tonight, will play *Hey Young World* tonight, and will play *Electric Boogie* at which point all the abuelas in chancletas and all the big mommas in slippers will come and *show these youngins how to really take it down.*

Biracial Hair

I have biracial hair
Pantene Pro-V waves on the top
Easy to comb, style, rock
until
I encounter my naps
I'm not talking bout them cute detangle with a spray
naps
I'm talking bout them slave naps
Like no comb, brush, or man
can handle the mess
I am naps
Like no way are you touching my hair
naps
Like back 10 feet up or we can dance naps
Those naps
like Damn
I have biracial hair
Those smooth satin silk threads hanging long from my mane
until you get to the back
encountering a jungle
in which you could find Tarzan and Jane
In the front you forget and relax in pleasure
until you reach the back
and remember pain
Baby soft baby hairs slicked back with that good 4-dollar Pomade
Yet those roots, and whiskers
entangled
soaked in the same olive oil
in the spaghetti sauce Ma made
I have biracial hair
Combs attracted as they run freely in my fine, breezy
splitting with most perfect part you can make
until it gets to the back and
breaks
Biracial hair like

Mama said all she could do with it was two big braids
and sometimes that was too much
so she left half of it free
Hours in the mirror convincing myself
I looked just like Alicia Keys
I have biracial hair cause
I have biracial blood
I'm not talking bout that cute they met and fell in love blood
I'm talking bout that slave raped six times
by the massa
birthing six mixed babies
later hung blood
I'm talking bout that cross burning in the mud blood
and you call me a mudblood?
Slit my wrists
My blood does not excrete in black and white
I dream in red
and in verse
like what dripped from
Emmett Till's lip
when he was killed for breaking down
color lines
Biracial who
never dares question
the story told
by her middle school
Biracial who succumbs to the abuse
of the kids in her middle school
Cause her lack of roots
had them calling her an Oreo
but her skin isn't that dark,
so more like a cinnamon vanilla wafer,
or a Milano, yeah,
that's more like it
A reversed Milano

I'm not fucking cookie
or a berry

My roots are deep too
My Biracial roots are not blond
or more than cotton soft
cause my blood
stood in the sun
picking cotton too
A thousand times discredited for my race
Discredited for my history y'all never get
cause there are no captions in textbooks about my truth
Let textbooks be your truth
and sprinkle the ashes of your ancestry into streams
I scream for a day, some place
where maybe you'll accept me too
Maybe we need to wake up and gain a fresh point of view
like something new
or maybe it's time for me to make up my own race
that loves my high yellow
barely there hips
no-cheek having
and biracial hair
Maybe I'll be green cause y'all people drove me there
My people drove me there
with my tender heart
tender head
and biracial hair.

The Border

My closest friend age 7 was
~~Spanish~~
~~Hispanic~~
~~Latina~~
~~Spic~~
Una angelita
who didn't speak
English
but knew how to hear my secrets
and keep them
I didn't speak Spanish
but neither did she really
Her tongue was
more a mass of mistakes
Tied up in twine
and spanked
Rode over in red ink
Swollen
from the bite down of her
front buckteeth
We'd sneak messages in
sand dunes
An ancient language
of silly putty
besos
and Barbie
There was nothing imaginary
about the way we connected
but our elders were always
tagging on corrections
We'd share clothes
until we were too grown to
share secrets
And even though
all the cute

was Polyester
shining gold
wrapped and strapped
I couldn't hold
Mother slapped my hand back
before I grabbed

on Fordham Road:
CocoCherryMangoRainbow
On 168th, Tamarindo
Empanadas con Bife, Queso y Pollo
Tamales Picantes! Tamales Picantes!
Mira, mami, tengo Parcha, Guayaba, Ananá, Naranja
Tengo Morir Soñando
(Don't you want to die dreaming?)
Mira, negrita, frutas frescas
con limón,
con sal,
con pimienta
Belleza, para ti—

I grew up thinking everything Mexican was hot
and burned. A stove
pot of flames
Untamable.
Casings of skin waving on a wire hanger
to be sold.
They have them in every color.
They are flavored salsa.
Too spicy, too peppery, too latex-y
and we
are a cotton-wearing people of quality,
I was told.
Tacky spics
and niggas
don't mix.
Not by flavor, food, or fabric
Not by feeling.

We like the sweet. They like the sultry—

We don't like those niggers in our country.
Sound familiar?
Casings of skin hanging from wire
to be sold.
They had us in every color.
We are flavored neckbone.
Too salty, too slippery, too monkey.
We aren't told
~~Those Spanish~~
~~Those Hispanics~~
~~Those Latinos~~
Those Spics
Picked
Cotton
Too.

Something

My nana has knees the color of
right underneath Heaven.
As if her mama had made her kneel on rice
every time she got fresh—
I'd rather be beat.
Her back is bad.
I bet her vertebrae look like crumbling stairways
or spiral stacks of matches.
Everyday on her feet.

Yes,
the electricity is out again.
No,
there is nothing in the fridge,
except salted codfish.
Boil some water for the rice and peas
and if there's cornmeal,
I will make you porridge.
Yes Chile,
I know you like it sweet.

When I had skinny ankles
I would hang them
over the side of her lap
and she would rock me.
Humming something I don't quite remember.
Something about being in the sky,
or being back home,
or being anywhere else but underneath my weight
and her own.
Her voice came out like a prayer.
Something silky and pink that
white girls wear in their hair.
Something soft.
Something desperate.

Something fragile,
but hard.
She sang like glass shards
and I wonder if it was them killing her.
Cutting at her throat every time I couldn't sleep.
Every Rock-A-Bye Baby.
At times, I would look her in the face.
She would look straight through my eyes.
It made me wonder if she had not died already.
What is she waiting for?
I am too heavy for her bones I believe.
She says I've filled out nicely
that I look like a lady and
how is this boyfriend she's so sure isn't good enough for me.
And I ask her, Nana,
have you died already?
Right under heaven looks kind of shady.
Looks like your knees.
Don't you think?

Something about black mornings.
Something about flying away.
Saltfish everyday—
so she sings.

And I boil the water for the rice and peas.

The Anatomy of a Fatback

The children are out back in the sun.
Aunt Juanita's torpedo titties hang precariously over a blue flame.
There is little distance between her face
and the sizzle
of 475° canola
puckering up to graze her collarbone—
A familiar lover.
It is the sound
that sends a signal
although Aunt Ruth prefers a smell
Aunt Sheila has a hunch
and Mama has always taken everything
at face value:
"I don't like the way that one looks.
Put it back in the pan."

Frying chicken is an art form
A balancing act
A tightrope walk
An origami folding action
of practice
and the Bryant-Butler women
are tenured
Masters.

Know the anatomy
of a chicken and pork
as if they have Masters
in the scraps
massas left after
eating his dry ass breast.

We never did like the white meat.
We always did suck the marrow
from the black bone

crack the fatback
between our molars
and squeeze the juice out
with our gums.
Soak the bacon with the greens
pull the meat off with our teeth
and chew the side of a ham hock
until there is more
Hock than Ham.
I am a pork rind hot sauce dipping
daughter
descendant of baby back ribs
dripping
Mama save the spoon so I can
taste it to the tip
You may say slow down because it goes straight to my hips
Don't give a shit
I double dip
I triple dip
Forget a dip
I'll take the pot
Eat all of it
My mama right
She put her toe, foot
ankle and
calf in it.
Chicken taste better with pork
don't it?

We are wide eyed
with our thumbs in the back of our throats
and our tongues at work—
The children marvel at
how black mamas
make slavery
taste so good.

Black Music

Sean "Jigga" Carter	David "Fathead" Newman
Is a blacksmith	Was a blacksmith
Before he is a musician	Before he was a musician
Is an alchemist	Was an alchemist
Before he is	Before he was
A lyricist	A saxophonist
And is a man	And was a man
Before God.	Before God.
His hands	His hands
A concrete trap	A dirt road
That dealt with death	That dealt with iron
And pulled night	And pulled fire
Up from the fire	From the night
Cracked rocks	Rocky and cracked
Made a match	Made a mismatch
Of misfits	Of melodies
Free style	Free.
Stood with	Stood with a
Marcy	Style
Beaten on the palette of his back	Beaten on the back of his palate
He spits	He blew
What Amadou did not die	What Michelangelo did not dream
But lived.	But drew.
Jay-Z was born	Jazz was born

Of a people

Who were forced to speak in a language

They did not think in

Who learned forgery

From the forgotten.

Dear Son

Dear Son
I bought a cake on your birthday
with nineteen candles and one for good luck
and I cried through the frosting
the cake is ruined, but
I'm sending you this candle
I paid four dollars extra for first class mail
so wherever you are
when you get it
light a match
or use a lighter
but light my candle and make a wish, Son
Make a wish
Promise
Cross your heart and hope to die
You promised you would write
and you promised not to lie
So until you come home
I promise not to cry
I'll be your soldier as long as you
promise to be mine

I've been thinking about the time when you were younger
and you told me you were going to be exactly like your father
You were gonna be a doctor and
you were gonna save lives
and you were gonna buy me that house that we passed on the way downtown
The one with the bricks
and the gate
and the lawn
And I told you as long as I had you I was fine as I am
And ain't nobody on Eighth Ave had a son more heaven sent
I told you that over breakfast eating chicken and grits
and you smiled and said mama

you put your foot in them grits
and I did
That was breakfast the day before you left
and I smiled like I was happy to see you happy
like I was proud to see you brave
but I know you and you're a baby
so I wasn't proud to see you leave
I know you
You're the eight year old who cried when he was picked last for ball
or scraped his knee on the pavement
You cried because I told you not to run
You cried just because I was right and you were wrong
so I threatened you with spinach and you decided to hush up
And I decided to buy you ice cream
You liked
chocolate hazelnut
but that Häagen-Dazs was expensive so you settled for
Turkey Hill vanilla
because you were trying to help me out
And we'd fall asleep on the couch
watching Terminator or something
and you'd drool through your Superman pillow
but I'd snore
so it was fine
I remember the time you came home from your first date
and you sat me down for hours telling me about your first kiss
and even though it was on the cheek
you said it felt like more
and you told me you were in love
with some twelve year old girl
And I was gonna tell you what you felt wasn't love
but I knew you had so much more time in your life to grow up
And now
I wish I told you all the things you don't know
but I'm not fretting cause I know you're on your way coming home
And I'm sorry I got these tears on your envelope
I know I said I wouldn't cry or worry
I'm sorry

but I just can't wait anymore
Because, baby, they sent me a letter
and I don't know what it says
but it's from the army and its U.S. first class mail
I beat the black off of you if you dead
You wanna cry?
I'll give you something to cry for
And the government can come and take you away
They can't hurt me no harder
They took my baby away

You told me you weren't gonna fight
You told me you were gonna pay for your college tuition
and help me pay for the rent
so you could become a doctor and save lives
You told me you were coming home
You sounded just like your father
and he ain't back yet
I guess you're like him.
You're a liar

I told you I'd be fine as long as I had you
And we would save every dime so we could live in that house downtown,
but how now?
You promised you'd come home
and you promised it'd be soon
What am I supposed to do?
Write me back soon,
Mama

1953 Cadillac Coupe DeVille

Behind Amsterdam
there are three.

One parked in front of the other
Bumper to bumper
Maroon, baby blue
and crème.
Lined up like finely dressed
acolytes
lapels pressed
shoes shined
Naps slacked back
and foreheads still glistening with grease,

all owned by one man
that I have never seen.

Maroon: meets Ethel where Flatbush and Dekalb kiss.
He's nervous.
Ethel is poison in pinstripes and suede pumps.
Ethel is sharp,
Ethel is slick,
Ethel is mean,
leaves him with weak knees
and no clue as to how he managed to serenade her sweet tooth.
He decides to marry her over Junior's
before he's even finished his plate.
He's smooth; Ethel on his arm
and keys-a-jangling in his back pocket.

Baby Blue: meets Ethel on the River,
and ain't she a pretty sight
with all the stained glass behind her.
She is shy, and puckers her lips warmly,
a spectacle for her mama in the front pew.

35

She harbors her zest
for when the car doors are closed.

And when those doors are closed.

Mary, Anne, Barbara and little Jimmy are conceived –
the latter of which was eager
and popped out in the backseat
right before they came to a deafening screech
in front of Harlem Hospital.
For that,
Ethel was grateful.
After all, it is said
Harlem Hospital has always been better at bullets than babies.

Crème: meets Ethel under the tracks
where he last left her
and brings her five long stemmed lilies
for each of her babies,
like she used to say.
Places them on her chest.
Despite his knees
gets down in the dirt
lays out the red checkered quilt
that had been in the family for years.
Unpacks the straw weaved basket
buttermilk wings and biscuits
sweet lemonade
specifically made
with a 7 lemon to 5 cups of sugar ratio
and a pinch of nutmeg
like she taught him.
He dines
with the most beautiful girl in the City
and probably on the east coast,
maybe even the country,
might be the whole world,
like he used to say.

And 57 years later
he was more in love with her
than he had ever been.
She was his bad Brooklyn babe
and he,
her prince. Her prince.
Her sweet Harlem prince.

Some people stop loving
at the grave.

But he
kept his love new
squeaky clean
like he first found it
in 1953.

Children

Adam says
he wanna be Jay-Z
Young Joc
Young Jeezy
Rick Ross
The Boss
T.I.
or B.I.G.
as long as he's Somebody
if it takes block hugging
or rock bottom
like his daddy.
Ishah says
Jenny thought she was from the block
until Jenny met me.
Ishah is three.
Got a dream to be
discovered
on Living Color
Harlem Puerto Rican Princess
and Senegalese.
Adam don't know what the east side of 143rd looks like
and doesn't care to see.
Kaseem
caught on the courts
of Morning Side parks
between two-fifth and tomorrow
maybe
a basketball baby
gives 23 a run for his money
in his 23s always running from his mommy.
Prodigies
the next Hova
or Kobe.
And Khadim

almost fourteen
says he wanna be the power his papa
steals from his mama
with a presence that
makes people get quiet
in reverence
says
I wanna be respected
not like Pun
or Pac
ball bouncing
or hugging the block
but President pops
off the lips quite nice.
2035
President pops of the lips
just fine.

Stage

My words can't flip flap for you today.
Can't tip tap
rabbit hat
no magic
tricks for you today.
I've had it with this stage
barren trick of a stage.
This was never a show
or a tell
tale.
It was Hell held and calmed in my palms.
I speak
here
You hear here
I heal here.

I've got no dance moves for you today.
No synchronicity
I am piecing together by falling
I'm feeling sloppy today
freely.
Judge me. Please.
Today I am your poet.
kindly.
You are my waves today.
I am in the center of the Adriatic Sea
An island with only enough space
for my hips to settle
And space to settle
around me.
Today you are my stars
I could never see in Harlem.
Hard to see anything shine in Harlem
except bars
and bling

cars and kings
Call them.
Suit is diamonds.
I am in on this sea
with my diamonds
looking at the waves
trying.
To sing a song my Nana used to ask
to the sky
A voice that could wrap me back to five years old
about God.
God,
Nana
has throat
cancer.
So I am speaking for her today
because she has cancer in her throat
it is blocking the sound waves
You are going to be her waves today.
We are going to do something big today
because the stage
has been the only place
where I can get God
so I need you to get with me.
Wednesday
she held me in her breast
she smells like bleach and sweat
heavenly scent
Held me in her breast
kissed me with her breath
and told me she hears
back home
people survive this
benign
or malignant
We can win this
He is the ultimate healer
He is the ultimate healer

So I need you to get with me
Waves
Stars
Space
Can we pray here?
I am thirteen here
with my elementary pleas
and silly poems about hair
Nothing hurt
except combs
and sticks and stones
Nothing burns like this hole
rabbit hole
Alice
I am
Where are my wonders?
I am not wonderful
so do not snap for me
There is no mystery here
Hear me.
The curtain will not raise to something better.
I am your poet today
kindly.
And I am not preparing for any big finish
I cannot disappear. Or reappear
Lock.
Or pop.
Dance,
but I can sing the songs my nana has
to God here
Because I can have waves
and stars here
And space surrounding me
and the Adriatic Sea here
I heard one of the most beautiful things
to ever set your eyes upon
Maybe here
God will glance on me

Are you stomping because I said something hot,
or because you are trying to get God with me?
I am hot here.
I am the center of Manau Loa
Hawaii
I am Giza
I am a lily hanging in Babylon
I am the lightening of Zeus at Olympia
I am the inside of Artemis
I am the Colossus of Rhodes
I am the sound of midnight at Alexandria
Here
I am beautiful
with a silly singing voice
that no one listens to
I am Luciano Pavarotti
under the lights
sweating
I can vibrate you
I can raise you waves
I am great
conductor of nature
I am sea here
I am Adriatic Sea
Here,
I am Peter of the Second Book
who did not
believe the waves would hold him
Who walked on water—

Will you hold me here?
Will you grab me up
before I give up?
Please?

They say its been sitting in her throat
for weeks.
But I cannot sleep

if she don't sing.
I need her songs.

God,
Nana
has throat
cancer.
Heal her here

me.

Beginning

When I was 8 years old
I picked up a pen
I wrote my first lyric
I read it to my mama so she could hear it
She called me poet
It sounded too possible to repeat
So I put it
placed it
neatly
like she taught me
to fold laundry
underneath my ribs
by my heart
and I promised my person
to prize that poet
That it was a gift from my mama
and belonged beside the
pottery she built
on my mantel piece.

Shooting. Stars.

I wish my hair was
longer, my butt bigger and
them sirens would stop.

Mating Call

In kindergarten, three-inch acrylic nails grabbed the collar
of my yellow button down, made no pardon for the scruff
of my neck . Dragged me and a pleasant brown skinned boy
six flights down to a dungeon. Opened the dragon's lair,
plump and plum colored with a steel club that smacked
the back of our palms. Punishment for having agreed to lifting
my skirt and showing him mine in exchange for him dropping
his Kente and showing me his.

At ten, pelvis sits like a laundry line when the air is hot
and frustrated, cocked to one side like the minutes running away
from the hour, and ticks. The corners are segregated, a group
of dirty white tees with long eager fingers swarm caddy corner
to a line of popsicle sucking caucuses, fresh in spring. I am told
that I will be his girl. I agree, even though he gotta big head, and
chicken legs, and all the others say he's dark as sin. We hold hands
for a fortnight, until he suggests we kiss and I find him cheeky.

Sophomore year, after confirming with my mother that the bulges
blooming above my ribs were not tumorous, I learn to move.
I've built a pendulum starting from navel to kneecaps.
For a summer, I snap my neck, roll my tongue, flip my eyes, tighten
my jaw, show my fangs as a rejoinder to:
slim.light.skinned.shorty.with.the.red.ayo.pretty. and, *bubble.butt.*
I forget my name.

Seventeen, the small bones of my hands knead and knock
his skin, dig and drum, make no pardon for the scruff
of his neck. Pelvis cocked to one side like the minutes running away
from the hour, and ticks. I am told
that I will be his girl. Other's say he's dark as sin. We kiss.
Build a pendulum starting from navel to kneecaps.
Roll my tongue, show my fangs.
I forget my name.

Punishment for having agreed to lifting
my skirt and showing him mine in exchange for him dropping
his Kente and showing me his.

The Comparative Clause

My love poems
are more social justice
Than your hate poems
are more of a statement
Than your complaint poems
Than your I am a political person
policy person
punctual, poignant person
poems.
Please.
Leave all the politicin'
for the politicians
and talk to me about
what makes you blush bright.
Is it pushing fists
or the way fingers fit
A delicate doily of pinky and pointer
The first five seconds between your lips
and his
The taste before the touch
or the didactic diction
of a hush
over giggles
which are louder Than your activism, your picket signs, and your protests anyway.

My love poems are bigger
Than the problems you point out in my people,
Player.
And I bet, whatever debate you have to throw off me
I can throw it better.
You can't hustle a hustler
especially one who is boss in a business like love.
My fight is a kick in the jaw
A brass knuckle lick

that hurts like a kiss
Stings like the lipstick she left
on the curve of your neck
to remind you.
I'm harder Than you'll ever be
because you still haven't learned to speak
softly
or how not to talk at me
or for me.
My sonnets beat your speeches
because I am in love
and you are indifferent
which don't make you different
but dead.

Speak to me in plain
because your jargon isn't as pretty as
your pain.

Hard Core; Track 6

today, i spent 30 minutes with a toothbrush,
and my eye pressed to the ground like bubblegum,
scrubbing Colgate onto the used-to-be-whites
of my Coach sneakers,
pulled out the Stussy
that i only don on extra extra special occasions,
shimmied my hips into a size six pair of denim
that i knew did not fit,
but gives me a tidbit of a booty,
decked out my wrists in every gold bangle my godmother has ever bought me,
flat ironed a flip in the front of my doobie,
spritzed two drops of my mother's expensive Eau de Parfum
behind my ears,
plucked my eyebrows,
drew a silver line above my lashes,
Blistexed my lips,
checked the mirror twice on the back of my bedroom door,
twice more in the downstairs bathroom,
and the fifth time right b4 i left.

i look hella good
and i smell hella good
and it's summertime.

i walk down Sugarhill, don't even bother with BX19
because i want to give my skin a lil time to catch some color,
like they say.
make it to the corner of Four-Fifth and Frederick Douglass
and while waiting for the go, get a couple of
God Bless your mama, Have a lovely day, sweetheart
and i just feel like a spongy piece of pound cake all hot
and heavenly coolin off on the countertop waitin to be bitten into,
but i flash my teeth and keep it pushin cuz i'm not sweatin them

anyways.

meet my girl on Four-Eighth
where Jerrie is finishing with her pin curls
then trek back up to St. Nick, cuz she didn't wanna walk alone, and

everybody and they grandmama is in the park.

it's loud and the air is steaming with the smoke of grilled corn.
we cut under the jungle gym to avoid the sprinklers
cuz i aint fittin to even give 'em lil ghetto kids the chance to frizz
up my blow out.

finally, make it to the fence surrounding the basketball court. and

there
u
go.

Adonis.
fresh with just ur wife beater on and all 'em lil chicken heads
know it too.
they got no dignity, with their cheeks all poked through
the wire.
waving at u and clapping when u score, and when u don't,
and even when u fall like
We still love u Boo. Groupies.

the sky turns purple in the funny way it does
and my girl say she gotta go home cuz otherwise her mama gonna
come lookin for her,
but she says we can try again tomorrow and i'm thinkin i don't even
have another outfit this cute
and i can't wear this same one twice.
the game is over and Queen Pigeon of the byrd pack
is all on ur ear with her phone out
and battin her press on eyelashes
smellin like the bootleg Fantasy spray
that the Chinese sell on Canal Street.
someone stepped on my sneakers so

i wanna go home.

i stop at Crown on the way and order popcorn chicken, fries,
two rolls and a Welch's grape soda and i'm feelin all pitiful
and silly and then
the bells on the door ring,
and i turn around,
and it's u
and u don't even see me
and u go to the glass and order popcorn chicken, fries,
two rolls and a Welch's grape soda
and the man says he don't got no more grape soda
and i clutch my heart cuz i know this is a sign from God
sayin that we r soul mates
and i have to let u know now or never,
so i breathe real deep, tap u on ur shoulder
and say,

u could have my grape soda if u want it.

u look at me like i'm from Brooklyn.

i don't feel pretty like i did in the morning
and u say,

nah, i'm good.

u don't say thank you, or that's real kind of u, or i appreciate it,
u don't say you like my shirt, or that i smell nice, or that i have
a cute shape or smile or that that chicken head back in the park
ain't have nothing on me or that u've noticed me b4 or that i'm ur
Venus. u say,

nah, i'm good.

And I walk home alone and look at the purple sky and realize we
aren't soul mates and you aren't so hot yourself close up in the light.

"A" Train Sisterhood

One:
You mark out your prey.
She is the baddest chick in the car
Her toenails are on point
Her baby hairs are slacked down
She smells good
Her skin is glowing
There are no
you've-worn-these-jeans-five-too-many-times showing between her thighs
There are no tracks peeking away
and she is smiling.

She is a threat.

Two:
Your nostrils flare
and your upper lip
curls open like a claw
waiting to pounce.

Three:
The once, twice, thrice over.
Start with the extremities.
Are her elbows ashy?
Is that a bunion on her foot?
Did she shave her underarms today?
Move on to focus areas.
Survey her edges
The chapped factor of her bottom lip
Is her chest sagging?
Is her booty tight?
Does she have a gut?
And if she does,
is it handled with a girdle?

Finally, the eye roll.
Start by staring just above the arc of her face
Check her out forehead to foot
then foot to forehead
Make sure she sees you do it,
but remember,
never make eye contact.

Four*:
Begin a light conversation
with a friend
Throw your head in subject's direction
every 3 to 4 minutes
Once she sees you
quickly turn away
and giggle.
Do not laugh
but giggle.
Repeat 6 times.

*Only attempt once you have fully grasped
the first three steps.

Five:
Is she with a man?
This step is self-explanatory.

Six:
A mother and her chestnut baby board the train.
Subject leans over to see.
Chestnut baby is bouncing
Clapping
Stringing together a sloppy sentence.
Scan the car.
All the women are at the tips of their seats
Their necks craning around a corner
to peep
Feel their cheeks swelling

into a grin
Stifled sounds begin to seep
between their tightly pursed
perfectly polished
lips.
Everyone looks around to check if this is allowed.
It is allowed.
Your hand involuntarily moves to your belly.
You catch the subject's eyes.

She is smiling.

Seven:
Smile back.

Daydream

Between the break
that rests like heavy, heat, and hate,
I, captivated by the sound the minute hand makes,
the numbers dancing dizzy,
the stanza sitting pregnant
between point nine nine of a second and zero,
lullaby of a calculus classroom,
yearn to escape,
to feel the Harlem dusty sunshine on my face.
I begin to lose.
Laying my head between my hands,
my mind opens
to a boy like a twirl of fabric
that wraps his way around my wrists.
A Valentine all sticky and lacey and pretty,
glued shut and kissed.
An ether of sugar and sour and pulpy pieces
to suck and get stuck in.
His mouth—a ball of caramel.
The creamy creation of an innocent infatuation.
His tongue—a maze of thorns
sharp, angled, and genius.
His mind—a mystery that never interested me.
I find myself
sinking in
to nights spent
sneaking out
or winding our whispers
in the crevices of my mother's
"good leather couch"
feeling grown
knowing nothing
and wishing to know nothing more...

Until the bell rings.
The minute and the hour meet
and it seems
I've missed the lesson.

Favor

I be so scared
and so crumpled tissue paper like
and all the boys think I'm pretty
and enjoy the shape of my mouth
like it is a mango—
sour sometimes
and yellow.

We don't match hues.

She fell green from a strange fruit tree
unripe
She's firm
Learned
to be ready
before she was due.

They cut a line
down her side
and I was the rock
that made her slices swole
She swallowed the excess
until I was clean
until there was nothing left
but a palm full of wood
to be planted.

She smacks the scared right out of me.

She keeps the backside of my knees
for pinching
When I speak tepidly
she laughs at me
She's not afraid
of nothing

Not even of all this fire I got
steaming
Not even of all these debts I made
dreaming.

She's done it before.

She's firm
Learned
to be fruitful
and broke
before beautiful.

She ain't cute.

I cannot escape her eyes
anywhere
I cannot cross the street without holding her hand
She's some kind of stalker
       some kind of shadow
That I don't want to look like
That I hate to look like.
That I look like.

Mommy.

Walking

He meant to say:
I never met a lyrical goddess
that uses hyphens and haikus
to prove that really
God is.
I thought Nefertiti was dead
and never wanted to believe
in queens
except Queen Bs like Lil Kim
Who etched the Milky Way on the small of your back
so Saturn's rings shake every time your hips sway?
I watched your walk uprooting the cement
and thought if only for a sec
the sun would finger paint my face
and you'd stop walking towards Mecca
Lady,
emit your soul in my direction
and I would lap Nazareth just to follow
and learn
But he said:
Ayo Ma,
Don't you know your curves tingle my nerves?
Let me rephrase,
you walking from school?
That means you must got good brain
and I would love to arrange some tutoring
And with his eyes I let him amputate me
Sever my shins
so when he wished I'd already be on my knees
Promising quarter plastic rings,
he proposed I squeeze a queendom
in one size smaller Apple Bottom jeans
and then I could really be wifey.
Told me God was missing me
since I fell from the sky

and while his metaphor was clever
I could never smile
cause every night till I was nine
my daddy told me I really was an angel
Every night he sang me flat lullabies,
he made me promise to always walk like a woman did
With the sons of a nation complacent in the crook of your neck
and the prayers of pigtailed potential up the side of your ribcage
like vines
Balance your children's infinities
on your hips
carry your divinity in your chin
and try not to trip
Walk hard, little angel
He meant even when bastards have tied your tongue to your soft pallet
and given you a bounty of Ebonics,
manage to sing.
When they've only written blues in your key
write your own melody
That's how a woman walks
So I sang the sharp harmony to my daddy's bedtime stories
Back when I used to hide candy wrappers in jean pockets,
now we hide condom wrappers
and Daddy, I'm scared I've forgotten your lyric.
Cause every song I start
it ends with shawty
and every time I walk someone calls shawty
We used to sip cherry pop
now we count cherries popped
Used to knock down piñatas
now by quinceañeras
we rock hips
Blast the treble on the track
show the small of our backs
There are no galaxies there
Our skin doesn't shine like a sun
but burns as if every shooting star we ever wished upon

lands on our laps
We used to claim ourselves as daughters of Eve
but I figure we must be a lost generation of apple tree serpents
since every time I walk someone wants to psssssst at me
Yo Mami,
Yo Baby,
Your mommies
Your babies
If you lifted your eyes from her breasts
maybe you'd see your sister in her face
and hear her heart trying to break free from her chest
I'm still walking
cause I promised my Daddy I'd never rest
He told me women walk hard
and I've been walking ever since
My feet aren't clean
I got corns for every corner I've ever been called pretty
and my soles are calloused for every step after that before
he said that he was only kidding,
but does believe that he has a bright future in my jeans
When I say my soul is calloused
I'm asking my daddy to re teach me those lyrics
or to the ten year olds on these streets that still hopscotch
but suck more than butterscotch
I implore you
Teach them back to these little boys
who play with rubber toys that teach them how to be soldiers
but never how to be fathers
Bulletproof vests and fingers gestured in silent Gs
We teach them how to be gangstas
so when they gonna find time to dream?
Teach them
what's limp in a hip
with a half-heart switch
is a woman
who cannot give any longer
I want to piece back the words to that song
Her body is sacred there

and his mind is stronger
But I can't stop to show you how to sing it
I'm too busy
Walking.

Chichos

He counts them like they are coins
flipping them with his thumb
I appreciate the way he covers his teeth with his lips
and nibbles
with his gums
Pinches them like they are cheeks
Bubble wrap for popping
Stems of grapes for snipping
Ganepos for snapping open
with his tongue
In his language
the bunches of baby fat
that time nor crunches
have managed to eradicate
have become
his private feast
A three course meal
Knots of satin
that he so likes to lose himself in
and never
never
come up
for
air.

In Love

I tried to hide that I was in love from my
Mama.
Love is hard to hide.
Plastered all over your skin.
This is
bands of coral
wrapped around my limbs
that I look stunning in.
That I be stunting in.

Yes. I be fronting. He is
something
sweeter than
just a friend,
Mama.

Sticky like taffy
slow like molasses
easy to get stuck in like 6 o' clock traffic
In love
can get you
in trouble
In love
don't like to hide
In love
is loud and obnoxious.
The fat lady who won't shut up
keeps smacking her popcorn
in the front row aisle
In love
ain't never been bashful.
Once it smacks you
it's attached
and won't back out
but backs you.

Tracks you.
        Tricks you.
                Tacks to you.
I tried to hide that I was in love from my
Mama.
Love can't stand to hide.

So.

Mama—
It's been a month. And.
I'm in love.

Joy

My cheeks
spread like Sunday
with a secret
With a smile peekers try and
snatch eyefuls of from behind
gapped fingers
I hide
and go seek with Day
in my fresh ass sneakers
She seems to have a snarl
Got her mouth all dry
and tied in a hitch
Not a big satin bow
but a braided rope
that burns your hands
but I got Tallahassee skin
Carolina skin like
my Granddad
and we don't rip, tear or break
easy
Believe me, baby,
dem clouds can't phase me
Not today
I'm floatin' way high
Sky, he be jealous sometimes
Think I got my nose all up in Air
and I'm too cocky for my own good
but I ain't full of myself
I'm full on you
and you
make my cheeks
spread like Sunday
with a secret
With a smile thinkers try and
analyze from behind their

clasped fingers
With something bigger than Day
Sky and Air
banging against my bust
And I think
I like
the beat.

M-18

Even when your bush has barely curled over
When your breasts sit on your ribcage like cinnamon rolls
rising slowly in a brick oven.
Even when church ladies continue to call you Sugar
smack your hand for yawning during sermon
and make you spit your gum in their scented palms.
Even when you still have all your hair gathered in bobos
sprayed with Motions
smothered with Shea butter
clipped with barrettes.
Even when you are most all parts girl—

                Heart is a woman.

A skinny ankled
  tight-lipped
wide-hipped woman.

She waits at a lone bus stop
under a no moon sky
holding tight to her paper bagged groceries
with a hard hard face.

Clutch

I think if I can
finally quit Black and Milds
I can quit you too.

Letter

I
think your words belong
alongside the lady
with the twisted lips
who men can't figure out
but women know all too well
She is struggling
Resists the fits
and night sweats
with a question sewn
in her brow
and breath
weighing on her breast like
a heavy brooch
She is so sure
She is unsure
She hasn't felt this before
so it's hard to figure out
It is more than the idea of you
twitching at the corners of her mouth
bumping behind the glass that
Mona Lisa is in.
Love
is the hardest thing I've ever
had between my teeth
without a doubt
and I never liked the aftertaste
Brussels sprouts
Stuck on a stoop
convulsing
spitting it out
Tummy aches
flip and trip about
I slip back down
this ground shakes when you ain't around

So forgive me for
saying
it ain't the sounds of your words I'd rather.
  You
can't send me no more sonnets
if they ain't all the way true
better not tell me to wait
if you ain't coming when you're through
Cause I'm scared out my mind
what you do with my heart
is uncouth
The way you grab, rip, and tear
I don't care if you're a poet
I've been here
way before it.
My walk ain't flawless.
Knock-kneed
I'm standing
Here's my hand
and
we can take this.
  Slow.

Vaseline Colored

Self-hatred is a real thing.
It's a boogie monster
breeding under your bed
and under your head
and right in between your eyes
if you let it.
For those who refuse to believe the Boogie Monster is real—
It is a pink slip
It is a plus sign on a pee stick
It is a gap between your legs
that you can't ever close again
A slender sliver of skin
that needle and thread
won't take to.
It is a black hole
And a blue hole
And a black and blue
hole to fall into
Ass first
feet in the air
and arms flailing with nothing
to hold onto.
It hurts more than a beating
A belt beating
A Billy club beating
A shoe beating
A just out the shower
palm-to-bare-back beating
A bleeding.
It is every color
It is brown
and white
Deep
2B wet and wavy
It is notblue

It is notstraight
It is nappy
kinky
curly
or whatever label you use to make it sound
less black-y.
For me,
It is Vaseline colored
High Yelluh
Transparent
It is stagnant
sticky
and stuck
Self-hatred is a sneaky mothersucka
It rides in unmarked cars
and stays on the corners of here
and everywhere.
It is at
everywhere you be at.
It pulls you over for
doing 5 over 45
For stacking 6 passengers
in the backseat
For lighting a bogey
at a red light.

Firstly:

I blame you for the recession for nine eleven for all them planes that been falling lately for what happened to luther for what happened to james for what happened to mike for what happened to teddy for what happened to my uncle for what can happen to his son for what's happening to all of us for all them 40s that been falling lately for herpes for cold sores for cold sweats for cold showers for when the hot water's shy for when the cupboard's dry for the moment of realization when you look to the side and ain't no toilet tissue left for left eye in the crash for kanye in the crash for whitney and the crack for crack for the discrepancies concerning crime and crack for crackheads in the winter for crackheads in the summer for crackheads year long for all these crackas comin to Harlem comin to the Heights comin to the Bronx comin to Brooklyn comin to Chinatown comin to LES for them contractors shipping us across the water like cargo to Newark, New Jersey for them contractors shipping us across the water like cargo to Amerikkka for the Trans Atlantic Slave Trade for the pillaging of earth for the thievery of this land from the natives and niggakind for global warming for the 2000 election for the Bush administration for Cheney for the Reagan administration for high fructose corn syrup in every beverage for obese 9 year olds for prescription pills and how they can eat out a family for all the earrings I've lost for all the socks I've lost for all the time I've lost that I can never get back for war for grown men playing with bombs for grown men playing with babies for haters hating for what happened to haiti for what been happened to haiti for nyc condoms nicking for nyc knicks trippin for pimps pimpin hos trickin for victims of oppression of degradation of corporation of gentrification of this nation and those across the ocean for Osama for Hitler for Sadaam for Idi for Omar for the ability to point for the ability to target for the ability to blame for shame for the rosy color that fills my cheeks when I can't say what I mean for his nonchalance with my nakedness for faking for fingerprints for bruises for bleeding for beating for allowing him to come over at all for silence and thick quiet that I could bite through for bending in ways my body don't bend to for the wackness for the WACKNESS for the stench for the sweat for fraudulent fairytales for cinderella for snow white for the one with the frog for petty princes with little swords for liars for lying for your face over his shoulder in my bedroom wall for the way my knee creaked open for the way his cold hands slipped between the crease of my calf and thigh lifted my leg to the side and crossed out your name in his clumsy script for this day when harlem has looked the ugliest that I have ever seen it.

Play

This ain't like chess.
There ain't no board
A backwards maze of black and white
pawns or knights
A one step Queen
A man's game of chocolate discs
to be kinged
Nor is there a hoop to swing
tip to toe in dunking
glory
Glimmering hardwood
floors to fling ones Jordans across
No screeches under sprinkling sweat
No stadium nor summer stretch
Beige tiles emblazed with the alphabet
where winner is
best wizard of Webster
A track to test
the fittest or whose
faster
A string of song to riff
and roll a chord as high
as summer ciphes
Ain't a race
Ain't no score
Ain't a ref
to read us rules
of right and wrong
There ain't no fakes or faults—

This ain't a game
I'm learning
but, Baby,
this is hard as hell

As hockey for brown skin
As finding one through nine
9 times up
and 9 times to the side
As scribbling in
100 words limited by length
and the trick of their fit
across and down
As hard as hiding for so long
found
don't make sense
is a thick sentence
that gets stuttered on
A tongue twister to get tied in
and slip
As a trip up of tenses
in French
As a rugby scrimmage
As scrabble against
Robert Pinsky
As loving you
start to finish-

This ain't a game
I'm learning
but, Baby,
this is hard as hell.

Hush

The disparity that blossomed
between the waves that midnight conversation
the ocean could not hold.
You carved a rift
with a horrid metal tool
like dentists use
below the rivers
and now
there is a gulf you think you can close with your words.

You cannot.
Your words are sand and the tide is hungry.

You say I've some growing left to do
Granted, I never disagreed.
There may be some things I do not yet understand
but believe me,
there are many things I do.
For instance,

1. I can't fix
the sun rises your five
for my six.

2. This is
hidden
After dark
After the streetlights come on
and we are expected upstairs
and tucked under
We are unexpected
A feigned slumber
You and I
A southern drawl
A mixtape

and a sweet smoke
sent
on this wind
to your window.

3. I do not care if you are in some way
compromised by this.
I do not care if this in your chest
makes you uncomfortable under the eyes of others
Oh please.
You've got my breath in a half nelson.
Deal with it.

4. Distance and time are little thugs
with water guns
whom never had mamas teaching them about
other peoples' feelings.

5. I am afraid
of the capability of your heart
The probability of its
falling hard
for some Megan lady
with a pretty smile.

6. Don't you ever dare
belittle this basket I've wrapped
in lace,
that I have secured with silk
Tied like a ribbon
on the back
of a pretty girl's Easter dress.
That I have left on your doorstep.

7. I am waiting.

8.
I'd
get
my
hair
wet
for
you.

This is dangerous.

So hush,
This can be wrong, and unrealistic, and un-kosher
and all that extra mess.
But I love you,
and there really ain't shit you can do about it.

Who Dat Dey Ring Dem Bells Fo'?

Who died today on Lenox Avenue?
Who dat dey ring dem bells fo'?
What dat paper say bout dem baby bits
dey carryin' down da street?
On da corner, someone
posted a picture of da chile
on pretty paper,
nice and neat.
Made a piece of a vigil fo' da deceased
tied ribbons to da bus stop
lit dem .99 cent Virgin Mary candles
we buy
at Dollar Century,
Whose chile dat is?
Whose baby dat was dey stabbed
until his lungs filled up like crimson plums?
Whose kid dat was lie in a mess of milk,
brown paper bags, and blood?
Whose little one ain't make it back
before dem street lights sprang on?
Who got shook?
Who got shanked?
Who got shot?
Who got blamed?
Whose sunshine went dim and cold?
Whose angel fell flat from da 18th floor?
Whose jaw dey left dere in the road?
Whose papa ain't ever comin' home?
Whose Moses is floating in da river
face down in dem waves?
Whose Maya been missing fo' 60 days?
Whose Corazon did dem workers find
in da back of dey green truck?
Who got beaten?
Who got forced?

Who got tortured?
Who dat is dat got tied up?
Who dat cried help?
Who dat cried please?
Who dat cried fire?
Who dat cried and
cried and
cried?
Who dat died and
died and
died and
died and
died and
died?

Shit,

ain't mine.

They've Cut Down All the Trees on Convent

Things crack
I've learned
I've heard things crack
Charcoals under a canvas of corn
Church girl patented buckle leather
clickity clack
A background beat to Sunday songs
Fire in the sky on every other night
other than the fourth
of July
Summertime
is a bowl of Bachata
A pot of greens
or gumbo
that crackles
Water on the sizzling streets
crackles
The neck of a brown girl chomping Bubblicious
between her teeth
pops and
crackles
Know,
I've heard things crack before.
The first time I heard a gunshot
crack and break
the lyric of an avenue
I ran
for
my
life
I don't know where or from or to
but I bet on my brother's back
I wasn't running back to that block
Two, where I ran lacked logic
middle of traffic

followed the rampant back and forth
a skill or sport sunk into the core of our hearts
If the hood is what you call home
than even if you've never heard a barrel spin and unwind
a lead plug, pushed by powder, sucker punch the sky
you know not to ask why
nor try to be a martyr or witness
You, like Harlem, dipset
like young daddies often do and
few don't, but most do
It is instinctual
to treat this ground like hot coals and hop around
Knees jumping to our chests
doing a two step
a toe wop
few folks
can keep up with
So I'm wondering when
they cut down all the trees on Convent
why didn't we dance in defiance?
When they came with their sacrilegious staffs of iron
what held us with our eyes wide, frozen for the first time?
That crack
was a wretched laugh lifted and splattered across dusk
like paint,
not the sloppy mistakes art and craft children
are entitled to make
but spilled like a stain
that ain't never gonna come out again
We stood, a tin can of sardines
Somebody's snack
Some suit wearing body's joke to chuckle at
That crack
didn't make us ask or run,
just look
watched them, masked,
lift and remove 200 years of roots
dry up an archive of sap

that blueprinted, brick laid, and mapped Sugar Hill
Tie down their branches
Butchers
Cut them, cuff them
march them down the Ave
A parade of their expendable assets
This ain't the first time I seen something tall and proud broken down
Know,
I've heard things crack before
But no,
never like this
Always the crack of a stomp trekking the block
away from crime from cops from each other
Always knuckles crack and smack against
skin precious skin young old innocent skin
Always the crack of a bottle tackling the curb
Always the crack of brown on brown
black on brown
black on black
The space that lives between the mirror and a face
The cracked cadence of
of resentment and hardship
Brothers, witness.
You are the killer and the victim
You think you are in a war
But who's winning?
Is it you?
For every body or bitch you collect by your fist
Who loses?
Are they playing against
or just playing us
Think on it.
What do you count as points?
Is it the cracks in your heart?
The number of times you hurt yourself
by hurting another
Shunning a brother, hushing a baby

cussing your mother or your god
hating the sky for its freedom
or a tree
for its capacity to stretch its limbs,
Heaven bent, past 145th —

If we let them,
they can cut us down too
but if we continue to cut down each other
they won't have to.

another poem about

harlem,
at once,
is a living lung
hanging from telephone wire.

a school of barefooted babes
stand directly under
on an intersection.
ashy knuckled
shea butter scalped.
enraptured
by its pulsing.

the drivers are coming
shining their high beams
and they don't stop for anyone.

i wonder,

how long can we hold our breath?

Thank You

God
Mama and Popsicle
Al
Miss Candy and Miss Yum Yum
All the Howards,
Butlers, and
Bryants
Tia Rose
Ishah and Khadim
Eileen
Grandma
Big Momma Jij—
for not never doubting.

Erica Fabri
Tonya Ingram
Michael Cirelli
Mahogany Browne—
for the countless hours.

Khary Lizarre White
BroSis Fam
Enmanuel Candelario
WWW Crew
Urban Word NYC
Mt. Zion Lutheran
Harlem World alldayeryday—
because it takes a village.

Zora Howard is a Harlem-raised writer, spoken word artist, actress, and activist. She is a member of the 2006 Urban Word Slam Team, which placed second at the Brave New Voices Youth National Slam. She is the 2008 first place winner of the New York Knicks Poetry Slam. She has performed at such venues in New York City as The Apollo Theatre, the Brooklyn Academy of Music, The Bowery Poetry Club and numerous others throughout the tri state area. Her performance work has allowed her to travel to cities across the nation and to the countries of Germany and Brazil. Her collaboration with filmmaker Lisa Russell on the short film "Biracial Hair", based on Zora's original poem of the same title, won an Emmy for Outstanding Advanced Media Interactivity. Her work has also been showcased on HBO, PBS, and NBC. In 2009, she was a part of the poetry reading series "Our Greatest Living Writers" held at the Nuyorican Poet's Café. In 2009, she was named the first ever NYC Youth Poet Laureate, a title that she will hold for one year.

The **NYC Youth Poet Laureate** is a one-year post awarded by Urban Word NYC and the City of New York. The program, a collaboration with Urban Word NYC and the NYC Voter Assistance Commission, honors young poets who exhibit a commitment to writing as well as a dedication to community service and civic engagement. *The program is designed to nourish and celebrate the vital teen presence in local civic engagement.*

Founded in 1999, **Urban Word NYC™ (UW)** is at the forefront of the youth spoken word, poetry and hip-hip movements in New York City. As a leading nonprofit presenter of literary arts education and youth development programs in the country, Urban Word NYC offers a comprehensive roster of programs during the school day and after-school hours and conducts diverse programmatic offerings in the areas of creative writing, college prep, literature and hip-hop. UW presents local and national youth poetry slams, festivals, reading series, open mics and more. All told, Urban Word NYC works directly with 25,000 teens per year in New York City alone, and has partner programs in 42 cities across the United States. For more information, visit: www.urbanwordnyc.org.